I AM YOUR
GUARD

I AM YOUR GUARD

*How Archangel Michael
Can Protect You*

ELIZABETH CLARE PROPHET

SUMMIT UNIVERSITY ⚜ PRESS®

I AM YOUR GUARD
How Archangel Michael Can Protect You
by Elizabeth Clare Prophet

For information, contact Summit University Press,
63 Summit Way, Gardiner, MT 59030.
Tel: 1-800-245-5445 or 406-848-9500
www.SummitUniversityPress.com

Library of Congress Catalog Number: 2008923280
ISBN: 978-1-932890-12-9

SUMMIT UNIVERSITY ☙ PRESS

Cover design by George Foster www.fostercovers.com
Some images © 2008 Jupiterimages Corporation
Image page 78: © iStockphoto.com/sumnersgraphicsinc

DISCLAIMER: No guarantee is made by Summit University Press that
the practice of the Science of the Spoken Word, meditation, visualization,
prayers, mantras or fiats will yield any person's desired results. The func-
tioning of cosmic law is a direct experience between the individual and his
own higher consciousness. We can only witness to our personal experiences
through the use of any suggested mantras or spiritual disciplines. The spiritual practices set forth herein are not intended to—and must not—replace
appropriate medical treatment or commonsense methods of self-protection,
including avoidance of potentially dangerous situations.

Printed in the United States of America.
15   14   13   12   11   6   5   4   3   2

Contents

PART 1

Prince of the Archangels

Grace's Story

To hear the call for Archangel Michael to come forth and protect is not unusual when I travel with my sister Julia. I've come to expect it. She calls on him for protection during trips, to clear traffic when cars are bumper to bumper, to help us find the correct address when we get lost. She even asks him to help us find a quick parking space when it seems impossible. Her calls are prayers given out loud with great fervor.

Personally, I feel the safest when I travel with Julia because I know that Archangel Michael is on our side. But I had never felt his presence so real until the night of September 22, 2002, at approximately 11 p.m.

That night my sisters and I were on our way home from shopping and a late dinner. Megan, my youngest sister, was driving her van. Julia (thank God she was with us that night) was in the passenger's seat. And I was in the back. All of a sudden a speeding car raced on ahead of us and made a sharp stop directly in front of our van as we approached a stop sign on a dark and deserted road.

The next thing we knew, some men had jumped out of that car and were pointing their guns at us. All I remember is a young man pointing his gun straight toward me— and coming up close to where I was sitting! I could see his mouth moving, but I couldn't hear a word. My sisters say that he was yelling, "Get out of the van!"

Inside the van, I had fallen to my knees behind the passenger's seat and I could hear myself screaming. In between screams, I could also hear Megan repeating over and over, "Oh, my God, he has a gun!"

In all this confusion, I heard Julia begin to pray and call on Archangel Michael to help us. The instant I heard her praying, I felt a sense of tranquility within me. I was still terrified, but her prayers gave me a sense of hope. "Archangel Michael, help us! help us! help us! Archangel Michael, help us! help us! help us!"

As Julia called to the angel, Megan un-froze from her state of shock. She gripped the

steering wheel and stepped on the gas pedal.
Julia continued to pray. But as we headed
away from the scene, we knew we were not
quite out of danger. We knew that the men
might follow us into our neighborhood. But
they didn't. And they didn't shoot at us while
they had the chance. They didn't even shoot
as we sped away. We were safe!

I truly believe that Archangel Michael
had spread his wings around us and protected
us from the evil intentions of those men.
Archangel Michael made his presence known,
and I thank him.

Archangel Michael,
    Thank you for giving me
tranquility when I felt fear.
    Thank you for giving
Megan courage to speed away
when she felt frozen in time.
    Thank you for answering
Julia's call for help.
    And thank you for spreading
your wings around us and
keeping us safe.

Your Personal Protector

Who is this majestic being called Archangel Michael? Have others experienced his presence? Will he also help me and those I care about? How can we bring him into our lives?

Out of God's own flaming Spirit, he fashioned the angels—extensions of his Presence that manifest in a form we can recognize. God created angels before he created us so that we would have caregivers. So tender and so present is the Creator's love that he makes it known to us in a most personal way through his angels.

Archangels are magnificent cosmic beings. They're the highest rank in the orders of angels, and Archangel Michael is the one to whom all the other archangels and their legions defer. Known as the Prince of the Archangels, he has millions of legions of angels at his command.

He often appears dressed in brilliant blue armour and surrounded by an intense blue and white light that looks like lightning. The electric blue that flashes in his aura denotes the presence of power, strength and determination. It also relates to the divine plan, or blueprint.

Each one of us is created with a cosmic purpose, and it's etched within our soul as an inner blueprint. Archangel Michael reinforces this unique plan, and he liberates us to perform our mission. With his mastery of the quality of power, this mighty archangel also teaches the right use of power—in government, the economy, leadership and all aspects of organization, administration and law.

But above all else, he is known as the angel of protection. All of us need to be protected, physically as well as spiritually. Archangel Michael is dedicated to keeping us safe, defending our souls and caring for us.

He has saved me and my family from serious harm dozens of times that I know of and I'm certain many times more. I can remember once when I felt the presence of Archangel Michael so strongly that I could not move my hand or my arm against the power of that stupendous angel who was protecting me from danger.

Sometimes people think that specific angels can only do certain things. But angels have a great cosmic consciousness. Though they have specialties, they can extend themselves beyond just one area of influence. So even though Michael manifests power and protection, he also brings healing for our bodies and souls. Indeed, in the early Church he was revered as the heavenly physician.

As a healing angel he frees us from forces, within and without, that intensify our ailments, our burdens and our karma. He assists us in overcoming the thought processes that conceive and amplify disease, disintegration and death. If you have a problem, perhaps some kind of detrimental habit, he can help to heal and deliver you from that burden. His healing proceeds from the highest science of the will of God.

 The Gift of Faith

E very archangel has a divine complement, or
  archeia. An archangel and archeia may merge
into one or they may act separately as individual
beings. Archangel Michael's divine complement is
Archeia Faith and she ensouls the quality of faith.

True faith encompasses more than the usual definition of the word. It is also the ability to maintain the concept of your divine plan, to establish your calling, and to be strengthened by the power of God.

Each of us needs faith in something, and we can have that faith in God and his angels. For people may fail us, but God and the angels will not. God always keeps his promises to us, even if we don't immediately see the answers to our prayers. They will come. The answers will surely come, though it may not necessarily be in the way that we expect.

Faith is the bird that feels the light and sings when the dawn is still dark.

— RABINDRANATH TAGORE

 ## Doubt and Fear Transformed

Many people doubt. They doubt themselves, they doubt God. Often they have a great deal of fear. Archeia Faith and her legions as well as Archangel Michael help us to overcome doubt and fear by the transmutative action of faith.

Michael has said that if we give him our doubts and fears, he will give back to us his full momentum of faith. You can say, "Here, Archangel Michael, take all this doubt and fear. I've lived with it long enough. I'll take your faith; you take my doubt and fear." Now, that's a good deal!

Michael is able to serve in a cosmic manner because of his own immovable, enduring faith. He has faith that he will receive all that he requires to fulfill his service to life. In fact, one of his roles is Defender of the Faith, and this includes defending the faith in us as well as our faith in one another.

Miracles Are for Believers

This is a story of someone who has great faith in the power of Archangel Michael.

On August 31, 1985, Kendra got up at 5 a.m. Something came over her and she felt in her heart the intense determination that this was the day that the Night Stalker had to be caught. She felt prompted by Archangel Michael that now was the time. Kendra started offering prayers to Archangel

Michael and she repeated them by the hour, dedicating them to one purpose—catching that serial killer.

The very same day Richard Ramirez, the suspect, was caught in an east Los Angeles neighborhood when residents saw him trying to steal a car. They captured and held him until the police arrived. Police determined that Ramirez' fingerprints matched those found in a stolen car known to have been used by the Night Stalker.

For more than a year, Ramirez had been on a rampage of raping and murdering. But he had never been caught, even with all the newspaper articles, even with all the prayers. What Kendra did that made the difference was this: She concentrated her prayers on Archangel Michael, determined in her heart that this was the day, and would not leave her prayer vigil until the goal she intended was fulfilled.

You may not believe that this was accomplished through the action of one individual who decided to keep a vigil. They say miracles are for believers. But you yourself will become a believer when you start realizing the many miracles Archangel

Michael will perform, for you and also through you in your prayers for others.

Sometimes it only takes one person with determination and faith to turn the tide of something that is very dark, that is malignant and that has persisted without resolution. When you work with Archangel Michael, that person could be you!

Reflections

1. How do you experience faith in your life?

2. In what areas of your life would you like to strengthen your faith?

3. How can you use your faith to extend support to others?

PART 2

Archangel Michael:
Yesterday, Today
and Forever

In Sacred Scriptures and Sacred Visions

The name Michael means "who is like God." Some say that this name is in the form of a question, the battle cry of the angels who defended heaven against the devil and his angels. They cried out to the rebel angels, "You think you are like God. Who is like God?" It's said that this battle cry became Archangel Michael's name.

A number of historical and scriptural accounts give evidence that people of various spiritual traditions have counted on Archangel Michael for protection. In earlier times, people had a much greater awareness of angels than we have today.

In the Dead Sea Scroll *The War of the Sons of Light Against the Sons of Darkness,* he is called the Prince of Light through whom God promises to "send perpetual help to the sons of light." He is known in Islamic tradition as Mika'il, the angel of nature who provides both food and knowledge to man.

According to Jewish mystical tradition, Archangel Michael was the angel who wrestled with Jacob. He guided Israel through the wilderness, brought the plagues upon Pharaoh, parted the Red Sea, destroyed the armies of Sennacherib and saved the Hebrew boys in the fiery furnace. He appeared to Joshua as he prepared to lead the Israelites in battle at Jericho. And *The Book of Enoch* notes that Michael commanded the nations. Everywhere we go, we find Archangel Michael!

Joan of Arc

Visions of Archangel Michael have been reported by many saints, but the most famous were those experienced by Joan of Arc. In the fifteenth century, he appeared to Joan and told her she had been chosen to help the King of France reclaim his kingdom.

At a decisive point in the Hundred Years War between England and France, when all seemed lost, Michael gave her the strength, courage and

determination to go forward. By the power of faith that Archangel Michael imparted to Joan, the forces of France rallied in defense of the flame of liberty.

Joan later testified before the clerics about Michael and his angels, "I have seen them with my corporeal eyes, as plainly as I see you."

Angelic Intercession in Tough Situations

When we, too, exercise the authority God has given us to enlist the help of the angels, legions can come to our aid in dealing with all kinds of issues, including war, hunger and disease. And we can assign angels to undertake special projects on behalf of our family, our school, our community, our nation. We can ask them to tutor our children on inner levels, to help us establish meaningful relationships with people in our workplace, to prepare the way for successful meetings. We can call upon angels to help us with anything— from the seemingly mundane to the spiritual.

A Powerful Push

One woman sent me this story about how Archangel Michael had helped her on a cold winter day. She had been visiting her parents in New England. It had just snowed, and their van had gotten stuck in the driveway. Her father tried rocking it, but it was still lodged in the snow. Then he pushed, with her at the wheel. Then they both pushed. Still no change. The more they pushed, the deeper the van got stuck.

After about a half hour, the woman, who is only five feet, three inches tall, convinced her father to get back into the van and start rocking again while she pushed by herself. Then she made an intense call to Archangel Michael: "Archangel Michael, place your Presence over me and push this van!" (That's how you speak a command to the angels.

They expect you to speak with the authority of your Higher Self.) In less than a minute, the van was out of the rut and onto the road.

The woman's father was perplexed. How could his tiny daughter have pushed that big van by herself? She says, "I told him it wasn't me. It was Archangel Michael! He looked at me for a few seconds kind of dumbfounded and then, in silence, got back into the van."

> *Make yourself familiar with the angels, and behold them frequently in spirit; for without being seen, they are present with you.*
>
> — SAINT FRANCIS DE SALES

Michael Brings Courage

Our prayers directed specifically to Archangel Michael can have a tremendous power. If you feel helpless in dealing with adversity, intimidated by others who seem overpowering, defenseless in the face of danger, call to Archangel Michael. See how he will come to your aid, as he did for Heline.

My husband was an alcoholic, a binge
drinker. He didn't like it that I was on a spiritual path, and he got physical about it. I was
really scared, but I wasn't going to give up.

   Then one morning I saw a blue light—
it was a beautiful aquamarine color. I could
feel this tremendous light, and I knew it
was Archangel Michael. And he said to me,
"You don't have to be afraid anymore."

   I stood up for myself and the fear went
away. After that, my husband was fine.
I stayed with him for twenty-nine years, until
he passed away.

Three Miracles

Here is another story I received about how
Archangel Michael came to the rescue in response
to an urgent prayer.

Most of us never fully realize how great
is the assistance of the angelic hosts or
how important it is to call to them every
day for protection. Sometimes we don't

*think of it until we're in the midst of an
emergency.*

*Such a situation occurred when I was
riding the Greyhound bus to Chicago.
Because of the crowded conditions, I had to
take a seat in the back. As always, I said
my prayers to Archangel Michael, and our
journey began.*

*At one of the stops before Chicago, an
intoxicated man came aboard. He was acting
crazy and his language was so profane that it
was difficult to be near him. He took a seat
behind me. I silently prayed to Archangel
Michael that we would not have to listen to
obscenity from this man, especially since there
were children aboard. Fortunately, he finally
fell asleep.*

*But the quiet didn't last long. When the
bus driver made an announcement, the man
woke up, and his language was as bad as before. He told the man sitting next to him that
he was going to buy more liquor at the next
stop so that they could party. He said he had
a great deal of money on him and started to
reach into his pocket. But the money was*

missing and he became enraged. He pulled out a revolver, yelling profanities and threatening to shoot if his money wasn't returned.

I immediately started calling, as loud as the situation would permit, to Archangel Michael and all the Lord's hosts to protect all aboard the bus and to bind the evil working through this man.

As the man was getting angrier, the tension was building. His gun was cocked and he was demanding his money, which he said was about $12,000. I called to the angels to help this man find his missing money.

Within minutes (which seemed like an eternity), three miracles happened. The first miracle: he didn't shoot the cocked gun. The second miracle: he found his money in another pocket. The third miracle: he started to apologize to everyone. It was as if he were totally sober and sane within minutes.

By the time the bus driver found out what was going on, stopped the bus and got to the back, the man had put his gun away and was leaving the bus peaceably, still apologizing.

I truly believe that without Archangel

Michael many innocent people could have been hurt or killed, including myself.

Michael and Your Guardian Angel

Archangel Michael is the guardian angel of the Lord who has served mankind for tens of thousands of years, and your own guardian angel works with him. So you can pray to both of them. You can say:

"In the name of my Higher Self, I call to the heart of my Father-Mother God and I call to Archangel Michael and my own guardian angel to protect and keep me. And I ask you, beloved ones, to guard not only me but also all souls of light in the world."

My Guardian Angel Helped Me

One little girl wrote me this story about how her guardian angel came to her aid just in time.

*I*t was a sunny day in springtime and I was riding my bike on a hill. I was only four years old and I couldn't get up the hill. I didn't realize it at first, but I started rolling backwards down the hill. Soon I was rolling faster and faster, and I was scared!

Suddenly I remembered what my mother had taught me about the angels and I shouted, "Archangel Michael, help me!" And soon I felt my bike stop. I looked behind me but I didn't see anything at first. And then I saw that it was my guardian angel who had stopped me.

My guardian angel was very tall and she had curly hair. She had a pink, yellow and blue shirt, and her skirt was white. Her huge wings were also white and she had a very bright yellow halo. I'm so glad that my guardian angel was there to help me!

Archangel Michael's Retreat

O ne of the ways we can commune with Archangel Michael is by going to his spiritual home, or retreat. All of the archangels as well as other beings of light that minister to the earth have retreats. They're located in the realm of light above this dense world—in the realm known as the etheric octave, or heaven-world. Each retreat corresponds to a landmark or physical location on the planet, and tremendous light is released from the retreats to the earth.

The retreat of Archangel Michael and Faith, the Temple of Faith and Protection, is located over Banff and Lake Louise in the Canadian Rockies. The temple is round and inlaid with gold, diamonds and sapphires. Encircling the temple are beautiful gardens, fountains and white marble benches. The central altar is composed of white and blue diamonds, and on the altar a brilliant flame blazes, ranging from a deep sapphire blue to an almost white pastel. Surrounding the altar are concentric rings of seats that accommodate thousands of angels.

Your soul can go to the retreats while your body sleeps. You can ask Archangel Michael and Archeia Faith and their legions to take you to their retreat and to protect your soul as you travel there. While you're in the retreat, you can receive instruction from these archangels and experience an invigorating spiritual recharge.

Often we don't recall when we have been to a retreat in the heaven-world. But sometimes we wake up in the morning with a vague remembrance

or a sense of a certain experience. We may think it was a dream, but many times it probably was not a dream at all. It was a real experience where we met beings of light, teachers, avatars, angels. And though we may not have a specific memory of it, something is going on at profound levels of our being. Portions of the experience may show up in our outer awareness as insights, new creativity or a deeper understanding.

Reflections

1. In which situations in your life could you enlist the help of Archangel Michael and the angels?

2. What assignments could you give to the angels on behalf of someone you know who is facing a challenge?

3. What would you like the angels to teach you when you go to the spiritual retreats? Remember to ask them for this specifically before you retire each night.

PART 3

Angelic Protection in a Challenging World

A Prophecy for Today

Everywhere we go, we face challenges and threats. We sense forces in the world tearing at us. We see the tearing down of our youth through drugs and alcohol, child molestation, teen sex. All of this can cause serious problems and interfere with the flow of light in the chakras, the spiritual energy centers of the body. And thus, for some of our youth their energies are sapped before they even complete their teenage years. It's the tragedy of our age that before we can even discover the truth to give to our children, they have already been influenced by forces that urge them to make self-destructive choices.

The prophet Daniel has provided the key for dealing with these issues. He received the vision of the coming of Archangel Michael in the last days. It was to be during a period of great tribulation upon the earth. I understand these last days to be the present time—the conclusion of a karmic cycle and a time of opportunity.

At that time shall Michael stand up, the great prince which standeth for the children of thy people: and there shall be a time of trouble, such as never was since there was a nation even to that same time: and at that time thy people shall be delivered, every one that shall be found written in the book.

—DANIEL 12:1

Daniel was saying that in this "time of trouble," we need God. We can't make it without him. And we can access him through his archangels, through Archangel Michael. God sends his archangels to be close to us so that we will know that he cares and that he will deliver us from all darkness.

Teens Count on Archangel Michael

Two teens got together to talk about their close relationship with Archangel Michael and how his protection has worked in their lives. Among the prayer forms they use are "decrees" and "fiats," which you'll learn about in Part 6.

Christie: There's a lot of danger in this city, so we often ask Archangel Michael to protect us. I know lots of people who get into fights, so I pray to Archangel Michael to keep me away from fights. Somehow I got to know these people, but they would never fight me.

I remember one time when I was in the sixth grade and I was walking home and stopping to make a phone call at a pay phone. A white van pulled up with four men who were probably in their forties. They kept on saying to me, "Get in the van."

I was so afraid. I was in a really bad neighborhood that had a lot of crime and drugs. So I started calling, "Archangel Michael, help me, help me, help me!" I kept on saying it as I walked away. The men

*in the van started to follow me. But when
I looked back, they were no longer there....*

*Last winter for two weeks I felt a pressure
in my heart to call to Archangel Michael for
my step-dad. I remember saying to myself,
"I don't want to decree right now."*

*But one day the pressure to give decrees
was especially strong, so I said some to
Archangel Michael. I found out later that at
that moment my step-dad was driving home
on the expressway when suddenly the wheel
came off his car. The car almost went over the
median strip into oncoming traffic on the
other side of the highway, but he ended up
being safe. After that incident, the feeling left.*

*Victoria: Archangel Michael protects me
from drugs. It's hard dealing with peer
pressure. So I pray to Archangel Michael
to free my friends from drugs.*

*Christie: Walking to school, I see people
smoking weed. People who were my best
friends when we were young are totally different now because they do drugs. My friends*

*come to talk to me about drugs, but I don't
want to do drugs. Even though it's sometimes
hard to say no, I know there's more to life
than parties, drugs and alcohol.*

*I'm happy for who I am; people respect
that. We always have someone to lean on,
whether it's each other or Archangel Michael.
We also give strength to other people.*

 # War and Peace

The dilemma of war, with all of its complexities, calls for divine assistance. Usually good people are positioned on every side of a conflict, and many are innocent victims. The problem of war and peace derives in part from the nature of life on earth. There is an age-old war of light and darkness on the planet. This war happens within our souls and hearts. It happens within families, in the city streets and between nations.

And what of the men and women who must fight the war? Many of them fight staunchly for principles, as this soldier explained.

All of us here will need every erg of light to survive the future battles, especially those soldiers who will lead the charge. It's in the nature of war that the toughest tasks usually fall on the shoulders of our youngest men. As every generation before them, they will do their duty, the vast majority with determination and vigor, and our forces will be victorious, praise be God.... Some things are worth fighting for.

Many soldiers have prayer support with networks of people who call to Archangel Michael for their safety. Parents, family, friends, church members—all get involved. One soldier, after his tour in Iraq was up, reported that because of such prayers his entire unit had survived. Not one of them was killed. He said he could feel the prayers. Another soldier, while stationed in Iraq, shared this remarkable story of divine intervention:

If these beings guard you, they do so because they have been summoned by your prayers.

— SAINT AMBROSE

Soldiers Survive a Deadly Ambush

While on assignment last week, we were ten minutes into the trip when insurgents ambushed us. They tried to engage us with three rocket-propelled grenades (RPGs) as well as small arms fire. Suddenly, one of those RPG rounds, carrying high explosive shrapnel, landed approximately seven meters away from our vehicle. At that short range we should have surely died or at least sustained serious injuries, not to mention that the explosion should have completely destroyed our vehicle.

Immediately after the explosions, the insurgents engaged us with small arms fire into their kill zone. Fortunately, since the vehicle was still operational, we managed to return fire to the enemy and quickly remove ourselves from the ambush area. We then consolidated our efforts and arrived safely in Baghdad. Thank God we sustained no casualties and didn't lose any equipment. Had it not been for prayers to Archangel Michael and his intercession, I would not have survived the

*ambush. My fellow soldiers are also grateful,
but they're still wondering in awe how we
could possibly have escaped unharmed.*

*The high explosive concentration used
against us normally has a killing radius
greater than fifty meters. We were well within
that radius and even closer to the point of
impact. At some level or another, we all
realized that our lives were spared for a
divine purpose.*

 # A Contrived Economy

Sometimes spiritual teachers tell us that we shouldn't be concerned about things like the economy. They say we should just be up on the mountain meditating and giving our mantras. But problems with the economy, including those that affect our personal finances, are significant even for spiritual seekers. For if we don't secure the abundant life, we may not be free to pursue a spiritual path.

Many of us earn our money by our work. So money represents the fruit of our sacred labor, and it is our lawful recompense. But we live in a contrived economy. Money is hoarded by those who trade in it and by those who control the world economy and the value of currency. This is not simply manipulating physical supply but, more importantly, manipulating the spiritual energy that is focused in that supply, which is the endowment of the people.

We can pray to God for the healing of the economy and to Archangel Michael to intercede. For we need spiritual intercession to be able to bring into our physical world the abundance and opulence of the light, which is available to us from the higher etheric octaves.

 ## Terrorism: The Ultimate Fear Tactic

The age-old promise behind terrorist suicide missions is that those who kill in the name of God will have an eternal reward. Thus, often terrorists will act anywhere they can. And we see the outcropping of terrorism in many ways, including the taking of hostages and shooting in schools.

Terrorism is the rent in the garment of government, society, institutions and individuals. When something strikes terror into your heart, it's like facing the living hell. It evokes the ultimate fear. And that is the point. Terrorism seeks not only to destroy the foundations of society but also to milk the light of the people.

Just as you imagine an individual wide-eyed with fright, terror opens wide the chakras, spilling light. So terrorism results in a spilling of blood and a spilling of light.

What can we do? We can give our calls to Archangel Michael and the legions of light. We can visualize the angels occupying every institution and every square inch of our nation and its embassies abroad. We can pray for the protection of our land and our people and for all people in all nations.

Reflections

1. How could the people you know benefit from having Archangel Michael in their lives?

2. What changes would you like to bring to the world through the help of Archangel Michael?

PART 4

The Battle
in the World
and in Our Souls

The Great Rebellion

And there was war in heaven.
Michael and his angels fought against
the dragon. And the dragon fought and
his angels, and prevailed not; neither
was their place found any more in heaven.
And the great dragon was cast out,
the old serpent, called the Devil, and
Satan, which deceiveth the whole world.
He was cast out into the earth, and
his angels were cast out with him....
Woe to the inhabiters of the earth
and of the sea! For the devil is come
down unto you having great wrath,
because he knoweth that he hath
but a short time.

—REVELATION 12:7–9, 12

The story of the Great Rebellion comes down to us in myths and in the world's religions. It's an explanation for the darkness, the evil, in the world.

I believe that this war in heaven actually happened, because I've seen the record of it on inner levels. I've also seen fallen angels and I know what they are like, and they are still in embodiment today.* They are often those individuals in positions of power who seem to be working against the greater good and the freedom of the people of God. They are the purveyors of drugs, nicotine, alcohol, crime—all that is contrary to the true law of our being.

The War on Earth

Ever since Michael cast the devil and his angels out of heaven, the war between the forces of light and the forces of darkness has continued on earth. Every day we can see the evidence of this

---

*See Elizabeth Clare Prophet, *Fallen Angels and the Origins of Evil* (Gardiner, Mont.: Summit University Press, 2000).

war on the battleground of earth—it's in the minds and consciousness of our children, our youth, our people and the entire planet. It is the warfare for the allegiance of souls, whether to a materialism devoid of the Spirit or to a spiritual path leading to soul freedom. The manipulation comes through every false doctrine in religion and politics that has been contrived to deny that God is in you.

 # The Battle for Souls

So the war that began in heaven is still raging on earth for the souls of our children and of ourselves. It is raging with such subtlety that people continually ask me, "When is Armageddon going to begin?" I tell them that it has been going on for a long time.

Look at our children. Look at what's happening to their bodies, souls and minds. This is the war in the streets of our cities.

When you see children who look as if they're

"gone" on drugs, as if they're wasting away and their eyes have almost no light, you might wonder, where has their soul gone? Where is that child you once knew who was bright, joyful and excited about life—the child who is now dark, depressed and suicidal?

This is a battle for souls. Destroy the body, destroy its chemistry, destroy the delicate central nervous system and the spiritual centers and you destroy the ability to contact higher vibrations. And so the soul is cut off from contact with the living God. That's what these illicit drugs do. They are death to the spiritual attunement of the soul.

We see this war in so many ways, not only in the production of toxic and dangerous drugs and chemicals but also in numerous other manifestations. And at a certain level, all of it has been designed to make the people weak and unable to see the reality of dealing with forces of darkness.

The best way I can see to deal with this equation is to call upon the Lord and to call upon Archangel Michael—the great deliverer of Moses and Joshua, and the one who fights the battles on behalf of the Lord and his children.

Conflicts Within

One of the ways that the fallen angels in embodiment attempt to destroy the souls and spirits of God's people is by accusing us for our imperfections and then telling us we can never rise again.

The children of God make mistakes. But the daily mistakes we make—getting into trouble and problems, getting so burdened and blinded by our karma that we do things we regret later—these are things for which we come to the altar and seek forgiveness.

And God does forgive you when you have a penitent heart. When you have a pure heart and you know that you wanted to do the right thing

Failure is not fatal. It is the courage to continue that counts.

— WINSTON CHURCHILL

but you made a mistake, you don't have to fear to confess that error. God will forgive you as a son or daughter, as a child of his heart.

So we don't need to have a sense of sin and a sense of struggle. Whatever we have been through, we can learn from it, and it can lead us to greater self-knowledge and understanding.

It is true that there are no free mistakes. Eventually, we will bear a karma for them in one way or another, though we can mitigate this karma through prayers and service to life. Nevertheless, we get to make mistakes without being ultimately condemned. And if we don't condemn ourselves, we can more easily pick ourselves up and keep on striving.

> *We often discover what will do by finding out what will not do; and probably he who never made a mistake never made a discovery.*
>
> – SAMUEL SMILES

It's not making a mistake that causes us to fail. It's making the same one repeatedly and not getting to the root of *why* that can cause our failure and be our undoing. But we can learn from our errors and from experiencing the karma they create. And then we can stop making the same mistake and we can move on. Sometimes it takes psychological work with a professional counselor to get to the root of the problem.

Most of us have internal conflicts, but we manage to cover them up. So often these battles are not fought and won by the soul but only left where they are. And the warring can be a festering condition within the physical body itself. Being at odds with yourself, disliking yourself, is a war, an Armageddon inside of you. Archangel Michael can help you to reach a victorious resolution of the conflicts within you.

 # By Free Will, We Choose

Often we call for angels to protect us physically, yet we don't ask for the protection of our thoughts, our words, our actions. But we can also ask them to safeguard these aspects of ourselves. We can say, "Beloved Archangel Michael, come to protect me lest I speak a mean word, lest I think a critical thought about someone, lest I spread negativity in the world."

And we can be aware that we have a choice in how we react; we have free will. We need to understand this for our spiritual path. If we ignore free will and that which is a corollary to it—responsibility for actions based on free will—we miss the point of salvation. The true meaning of salvation is self-elevation to the consciousness of our Higher Self. By free will, we make those choices that move us closer to that consciousness.

God does not compel the will: rather He sets the will free, so that it wills not otherwise than what God himself wills.

— MEISTER ECKHART

By free will we choose whom we will serve, whether we are going to be one with God or whether we are going to be human gods—those who use God's energy only for the lesser self. It is the great gift of free will that we can choose to use God's energy to become one with our Higher Self.

Every day there are split seconds in our life when we make decisions. Are we going to indulge in that little bit of gossip? Are we going to indulge in criticism of someone else? Are we going to indulge in a point of pride or irritation?

When we make the decision to do so, we are no longer aligning ourselves with God and his living Presence within us. At that point, we are aligning ourselves with negativity, with forces who have come to defeat us, sometimes ever so subtly; and it can be very subtle. But we can invoke the assistance of Archangel Michael to guard our consciousness and to help us make the best decisions.

 # Call for Spiritual Help

So in the world there is a battle of Armageddon, and within ourselves there is often a battle. We can see the players and we can see how they outpicture choices. We can see before our very eyes the consequences in the lives of those who make wrong choices, and we can say, "There but for the grace of God go I. Help me, O God. And help me to assist others as they strive to make the best decisions in exercising their free will. Guide, guard and direct us all, that we might make those choices that will bring us closer to our Higher Self."

Pray to Archangel Michael for protection for yourself, for those you know and those you love. And call to him to deliver all who are immersed in the battle of Armageddon at any level of their being.

Reflections

1. Notice how and where you experience internal conflict. How can Archangel Michael help you to reach a victorious resolution?

2. What other steps could you take to lessen and resolve inner conflict?

3. In what ways could you use free will to draw closer in consciousness to your Higher Self?

PART 5

Communing with God and His Angels

Does God Always Answer Prayer?

Whenever you call to the angels in God's name, they must answer, as long as your call is consistent with divine will and it does not cause injury to life. Sometimes you assess a situation and you feel that it's hopeless, that not even the angels can help you. But this is precisely when you need to give your prayers. And then surrender the situation to the will of God.

Sometimes people are rescued, sometimes they are not. It depends on their karma and God's will for them, and we don't know what that is. But one thing is certain—our call will compel God's answer and the maximum amount of mercy his law will afford. More than that we cannot expect, for God doesn't break his laws. He doesn't break the law of karma, and everyone has karma.

We need to experience our karma because it teaches us things we need to learn for our spiritual growth. Sometimes when we go through injury and pain, for instance, it softens our heart. We become more humble. God teaches us in many ways, and whatever these are we can always be grateful.

Michael's State Troopers

The following story shows how some of my students learned an unexpected lesson when they were praying to Archangel Michael.

It happened one day when I was traveling through Oregon on a bus with a group of them. We were praying to Archangel Michael when all of a sudden we heard over a loudspeaker, "Pull over to the side of the road."

And there they were, the state police of Oregon. Two state troopers got out of their car, and our driver got out and began talking with them. They said, "Did you know how fast you were going around that curve? You passed about five cars." And our driver said, "No, I really didn't know." So the officer said, "Well, you were doing 65 around that curve, passing all those cars. I'm going to have to give you a ticket."

The students wondered, when we had been asking Archangel Michael for protection, how could he possibly have allowed us to get a ticket? I explained that Archangel Michael represents God's will and his law. So the police, in their position of keeping the law, are in his domain. The police forces throughout the world are intended to serve under Archangel Michael to maintain the law and protect the people.

These state troopers were doing their duty. A lot of people on the road were speeding. It seemed that nobody was observing the speed limit. But we magnetized the enforcement of the law by our prayers to Archangel Michael.

I told the students that when you intensify an action of light in your consciousness, you intensify that action on all planes. When you call to Archangel Michael and his legions, you're invoking the law. So it's a good idea to be in harmony with the law—the law of both God and man. Therefore, if you're going to invoke the law, you'd better be sure you're obeying the law!

I was happy to make a contribution to the state

of Oregon by paying the fine because I knew that this experience was a good lesson for everyone.

 ## The Divine Exchange

True devotion is a tangible current of divine love sent from your heart to God's heart. Through that love, you create a cord that ties you to God and to all the heavenly beings to whom you pray. On the return current, God sends you a reinforcement and multiplication of that love according to the quality and qualification of your communication. You may feel God's response as his warmth and compassion or some other manifestation of his light.

But you cannot receive from God any more light than you can protect and hold in harmony. You can do everything you know to do on the spiritual path, but if you cannot hold fast what you receive from God, he will not increase it. So you can invoke Archangel Michael's assistance to help you guard that light.

Talking with God

Prayer begins with communion as a personal and intimate conversation with God. I invite you to develop the habit of communing with God, of talking with him. It takes coming apart from the world, becoming quiet. God wants to talk with us about our problems, but we need to initiate the connection.

> *God speaks in the silence of the heart. Listening is the beginning of prayer.*
>
> — MOTHER TERESA

When we commune with our Higher Self, we open the way for the limitless flow of God's light and, with it, the answers to our prayers. To understand these answers, we put ourselves in a state of attunement and receptivity to God. And we need to be receptive to God when he says no as well as when he says yes.

God is not a Santa Claus whom we go to only for favors. Those who experience answered prayer are those who realize that God expects us to give him something. It can be in the form of service to his children, love, music, and so forth. Everything we do in our daily life can be done for God; it can be a gift of ourselves to him. Then when we have a need, we already have a momentum of interchange. When we serve the light and continue to serve the light, the light will serve us.

 ## Your God-Identity

When we think of communing with our Higher Self, we may wonder, "Who is my Higher Self?" And most of us, from time to time, have asked ourselves, "Who am I?" My husband, Mark Prophet, addressed that question like this:

Before the redwood trees, before the rocks, before our physical form, before our sense of separation, God was. God the Spirit was the creator of the manifestation—man. Man is not at all separate from God. But man

*supposes himself to be separate because he
does not feel big enough to become one
with God.*

*You are just as much a part of God today
as any of the masters and saints in heaven.
God is really what you are. But people say,
"Well, if I'm God, why don't I act like God?"
So I want to get across the concept of the soul.*

*The soul is a vital potential, a potential of
the Spirit of God in you. That potential is
there. The question is, what are you doing
with it? Is it staying small, or is it becoming
buoyant and reaching out for more of what
God has already promised it? The greatness
and potential that is in some of the great
adepts and masters is also within the realm of
your own doing if you will recognize it.*

The Chart of Your Divine Self on page 62 illus-
trates your vast spiritual potential and destiny. It is
a portrait of you and God within you. The upper
figure is your "I AM Presence," the Presence of
God that is individualized for each of us.

The middle figure represents your Higher

THE CHART OF YOUR DIVINE SELF

Self—your inner teacher, voice of conscience and dearest friend. Jesus discovered the Higher Self to be "the Christ" and Gautama discovered it to be "the Buddha." Thus, the Higher Self is sometimes called the Inner Christ (or Christ Self) or the Inner Buddha. Christian mystics sometimes refer to it as the inner man of the heart or the Inner Light. And the Upanishads mysteriously describe it as a being the "size of a thumb" who "dwells deep within the heart." Whether we call it the Christ, the Buddha, the Atman or the Tao, each of us is meant to become one with our Higher Self.

The lower figure represents you on the spiritual path, surrounded by the protective white light of God and the violet flame, a high-frequency spiritual energy.

Surrounding the I AM Presence are seven concentric spheres of light that make up what is called the causal body. Each sphere denotes a different aspect, or quality, of cosmic consciousness that you have developed throughout your lifetimes. These attributes determine your individual gifts and talents, which you can draw down from your causal body.

The ribbon of white light descending from the heart of the I AM Presence through the Higher Self to the lower figure is the crystal cord. It is the umbilical cord, or lifeline, that ties you to Spirit. This stream of spiritual energy nourishes and sustains the flame of God within your heart, which is your soul's potential to be one with God.

God has so loved us that he has placed this flame within us as a portion of himself to which we have recourse. This divine spark is our point of contact with God.

Archangel Michael serves on the blue ray—the ray, or God flame, of the outermost sphere of the causal body. It relates to the qualities of power, will, faith, protection, direction, courage and obedience. It correlates to a spiritual energy center within your body, the throat chakra. This is your power center, and it gives you the power of the spoken word. When you use it to bless life, to instruct, to heal—in positive expressions—that sphere of your own I AM Presence increases in size. Likewise, the other spheres also increase as you express the attributes related to them. Thus, you grow in attainment and in the manifestation of your Real Self.

 Listening for the Inner Voice

Being receptive to God means listening to the inner voice. This voice, which men call conscience, is living proof that God as a Person, our Higher Self, lives within us and is speaking to us. The voice of our Higher Self leads us back to our true reality. It is always with us and gives us unerring guidance.

A marvelous habit to instill in children as well as in ourselves is to be listening for the inner voice, which is also known as our own guardian angel. If you can't yet tell the difference between the inner voice and those voices that are lower forms of consciousness, just do the best thing you know how to do, the thing that's nearest to what seems right at the time. The more you practice obeying

the inner voice, the more you will hear it conveying the next step on the path.

An Angel's Love

This is a story about a child who heard and
obeyed the inner voice, and thereby she was spared
from what could have been great harm.

*I was about ten or eleven years old. It was
a hot summer day and my father had just
picked up my sister and me from our summer
camp, and we were driving home. I was so
sleepy that I thought it would be wonderful
to lean my head up against the car door and
fall asleep.*

Just then I heard a voice I shall never

*forget. It was a
female voice—firm
yet gentle, command-
ing yet soothing.
The voice spoke to
me and said: "No,
do not lay down
your head. Wait until*

you get home."

I do not have the words to describe the beauty of this voice nor the depth of this being's care for me. Such is an angel's love. I instantly obeyed her command and raised myself to a more upright position.

Seconds or minutes later, our car was hit broadside by another car, and the side on which I was sitting was completely smashed in. If I had laid my head down as I had intended, I might have incurred severe head injuries and perhaps died. My gratitude to God for the wondrous intercession and devotion of the angels of light.

The Power of the Name of God

People everywhere, from every walk of life and many religions, have used the spoken word in their devotions, often repeating mantras by the hour to draw down the light of God. We, too, can offer prayers to anchor the light, using God's name to do so.

When Moses beheld the burning bush, he asked the angel of the Lord, "What is thy name?" The Bible records that God said, "I AM THAT I AM. . . . This is my name for ever, and this is my memorial unto all generations."

This sacred name of God is the key whereby we bring down the light from above. When we say I AM THAT I AM, we are affirming, "I AM here below that which I AM above. God is where I am."

Between the humble and contrite heart and the majesty of Heaven there are no barriers. The only password is prayer.

— HOSEA BALLOU

God gave us the gift of his name and his personal Presence with us, our I AM Presence. Each time you say, "I am," you are saying the name of the Presence of God with you. Whatever you follow it with becomes affirmed and confirmed by the power of that name. If you say, "I am sick and tired and old," so it is, because you have decreed it by the name of God. But if you say, "I am joyous, I am happy," then the light descending to you is qualified with the joy and happiness of God.

The Precision
of the Light

Many people don't want to name negative conditions, but it's often the next best step on the path of overcoming. Long ago I had a teacher who said that we have to name error in order to get at it and deal with it.

Sometimes I may feel a burden upon me but I don't know the source of it. So I call to God to make it known to me. Until I know what it is, I may pray generally all day and the burden may or may not be lifted and it could take any amount of time. But when I know the exact cause and I make a specific call on it, that weight is sometimes lifted instantaneously.

Therefore we name specific conditions in our prayers so that the angels can act with precision. Each word carries a unique vibration. So when we pronounce a word, we are conveying that vibration as well as the thoughtform of what we are naming. And we are saying to the angels, I am giving you the authority to act on this particular condition. We are communicating vibrationally by the word to the Godhead, and the light goes into that situation.

Some of the problems for which we would pray may be the result of past sowings that we are now reaping. Some may stem from habits of consciousness, such as worry, concern, inharmony, irritability. And our attitude toward life can also cause problems. Others may come from a long momentum of difficulties.

But no matter what the cause, we can approach all problems in the same way—by knowing that the light is greater. Increasing light always comes from prayer. Scientific prayer, as dynamic decrees, helps us to be all light.

Reflections

1. In what ways has God answered prayer in your life?

2. There is great power in the words "I am." What changes would you make in what you affirm about yourself? And in what you affirm to others about themselves?

3. In what way do you hear the guidance of your Higher Self and the angels?

PART 6

Invoking Heavenly Assistance

The Creative Power of Sound

Scientists Hans Jenny and Masaru Emoto have shown by their experiments that different sounds produce different impressions on matter. Sound is the universal force of creation. Sound creates impression on matter; silence does not.

When God created the world, he spoke: "Let there be light." He didn't just meditate; he spoke. And instantaneously, the light of Spirit, which always was, is and ever shall be, was manifest as matter.

We have the authority of God, we who are his sons and daughters, to speak the Word. Through speech, we communicate and receive each other's messages directly. If we sat in silence, we might get an

Prayer is naught else but a yearning of soul.... When it is practiced with the whole heart, it has great power.

— MECHTHILD OF MAGDEBURG

awareness of one another's thoughts, but we would not get the full power of the communication and the full transfer.

So spoken prayer can be more effective than meditation or silent prayer because of its ability to change matter. We're in a matter universe. Matter is substance, and the wrong arrangement of substance, in a sense, is the real definition of all of our problems. So we want to rearrange substance —whether it's a physical illness or an absence of money in our pocket or a lack of education, etc.

 ## Effective Spoken Prayer

Two spoken prayer forms that are effective in summoning angelic help are decrees and fiats. Decrees are dynamic prayers or affirmations that enable you to direct God's energy into the world for constructive change. Fiats are short, powerful decrees. Whenever possible, it is most effective to speak your decrees and fiats out loud in a strong, firm voice.

The power of your calls is greatly amplified

by visualization. A simple method of visualizing Michael's blue flame or any other God-flame is to concentrate on the memory of a blazing campfire. See the image of the physical flames take on the color of the flame you desire to invoke. Now enlarge your inner vision of the flames to fill your entire consciousness. Then visualize these flames enveloping the people or situations about which you are praying.

Making Your Prayers Personal and Powerful

To invoke the name of God as you begin your devotions, you may want to use the following preamble or simply speak a personal prayer from your heart. You can include the names of the heavenly beings to whom you are calling. After giving any preamble one time, you can give one or more decrees as many times as you like.

"In the name of the I AM THAT I AM, I call to you, beloved Archangel Michael, and your legions of blue-flame angels. I ask you to ___[personal prayer]___. To this end, I decree: ... "

After a decree is given, it is sealed with a closing. This is your acceptance that your calls have been received in the heart of God and that God will answer. It seals the action of precipitation that causes the light from Spirit to descend tangibly into matter. You might give a closing like the following:

"I ask that my call be multiplied and used for the assistance of all souls on this planet who are in need. I thank you and I accept it done this hour in full power, according to the will of God."

 ## Calling to Michael and Legions of Light

The decree "Traveling Protection" summons Archangel Michael, and he comes with his legions of angels. When you're driving to work, you can give this decree to Archangel Michael and ask him to place himself around your car and around every other car on the road. You can extend his protection to everyone who is using any form of transportation anywhere in the world. You can give this decree wherever you are, anytime, anywhere, whether you're traveling or not.

Visualize Archangel Michael all around you, guarding you in every direction. Visualize his armour as the invincible light of God coalesced as fiery diamonds and blue sapphires. See this powerful, majestic archangel "cutting you free" with his spiritual sword of blue flame from addictions, burdens, limiting habits.

If you truly want to be free, pray fervently every day to Archangel Michael and ask him to deliver you. If you want to stop smoking, drinking or overeating, if you want to get drugs out of your system, if you want to get your life in order so you can serve God better, call to Michael so that he can assist you in overcoming these burdens.

Archangel Michael is as big as the earth and as tiny as a cell. You can call to Michael and his legions to enter your body, even your cells, with their swords of blue flame to help arrest whatever physical problem you are having.

*The sword of blue flame of Archangel Michael is an
action of the spiritual fire. Archangel Michael literally takes
his sword and cuts around our form and beneath our feet.
The blue-lightning angels who go forth from Banff use this
sword to cut people free from danger, from darkness and
from whatever they want to be delivered.*

You can give the "Traveling Protection" decree
for your family, friends and co-workers. You can
give it for the whole world. Be creative and
thoughtful in your prayers, and speak from your

heart. Before you give this decree, you can offer a preamble like the following.

Lord God Almighty, in thy name I AM THAT I AM, send Archangel Michael and his legions of light to seal me in the blue flame of God's holy will and protection. Legions of light, wield your swords of blue flame to cut free my children, my family, my community, city and nation, all people. Protect us from all harm known or unknown. Seal us in the light of God. To this end, I decree:

Traveling Protection

Lord Michael before,
Lord Michael behind,
Lord Michael to the right,
Lord Michael to the left,
Lord Michael above,
Lord Michael below,
Lord Michael, Lord Michael wherever I go!

I AM his love protecting here!
I AM his love protecting here!
I AM his love protecting here!

A Flat Tire Mysteriously Inflates

The following is a story about someone who experienced a remarkable improvement in her situation after she gave this decree to Archangel Michael.

I walked to my car in the parking lot in order to return to west Los Angeles, where I was living at the time. My left rear tire was completely flat. I was very frustrated with myself because for more than three weeks I had been driving without a spare. "I'll take care of it tomorrow," I kept saying.

It was 11:00 p.m. on a Saturday night, no one was around, and I had twenty-five miles to go. I got in the car and started to drive, trying to think about my options. The car was making this clunking sound as I drove slowly and headed toward the highway. The sound of the wheel was so bad that I pulled over to look at it. When I saw the tire, my heart sank. I would just have to drive very slowly and pray that it would last long enough for me to get help.

At that moment, I remembered the call "Lord Michael before, Lord Michael behind...." I said to myself, "Maybe, if I just start saying that mantra as fast as I can, I'll be able to think of some solution to this mess even though the problem was entirely due to my procrastination." I kept verbally kicking myself for not having gone to get my spare tire.

It was now about 11:15 p.m., and things were not going to improve if I just sat there. I knew I needed some kind of miracle, but I truly felt in a state of near total despair. My unspoken prayer to Archangel Michael was just to get me down the hill safely. I didn't really care if the tire was destroyed in the process.

Feeling depressed and not very confident, I began to say the decree but not very loudly. I hadn't said it more than a few times when I began to hear a soft hissing sound coming from the left rear of the car. And I felt a very subtle but distinct lifting of that part of the car. My first thought was to get out and see what was going on. But something told me to just stay put and keep repeating the decree as fast and as loudly as I could. So that's what I decided to do.

As I was driving, I noticed that the clunking had disappeared. I felt that what was actually happening could not possibly be happening, but I knew it was happening! I kept listening for the clunking sound of the tire as my car picked up speed, and the sound was not there. I was driving at 50 mph nearly yelling the call to Archangel Michael over and over.

As the car was coming down the final hill, suddenly the tire went flat again and started clunking. I drove the last mile very slowly and pulled into the gas station. The man said that he did not have a spare tire which would fit my car and that his equipment was not working.

I stood there for a minute and then decided, "Look, the mantra to Archangel Michael got you safely this far. Do it again

*and see if it'll do anything." Within a few
minutes the man came out and said, "You
know, I think I can fix your tire." He did it
in ten minutes and I was on my way home.*

*During the years since this incident, I have
asked myself, "Did that really happen?"
I know that it did. The only way I got down
that hill safely was through the intercession of
Archangel Michael.*

*I go back to this experience and realize
that this was only one of countless times he
has stepped in for me personally. I have not
seen him with my physical eyes, but I know
his presence in my life.*

The decree "I AM Presence, Thou Art Master"
is a key affirmation of the one God. We can begin
by invoking God's name; then we speak the decree.

When you give this decree, visualize yourself
within a cylinder of light. The Presence of God, to
whom you are calling, is also in his archangels. So
with this call, you also have the protection of
Archangel Michael, and a cylinder of his blue
flame protection descends around you.

In the name of God, I AM THAT I AM:

I AM Presence, Thou Art Master

I AM Presence, Thou art Master,
I AM Presence, clear the way!
Let thy light and all thy power
Take possession here this hour!
Charge with victory's mastery,
Blaze blue lightning, blaze thy substance!
Into this thy form descend,
That perfection and its glory
Shall blaze forth and earth transcend!

Boldness of Intention

When you're dealing with a serious problem like drugs, you're not just wrestling against the substance and the habit, with its toxicity. You're also dealing with unseen forces reinforcing the addiction. That's why addictions are so hard to break.

Call upon the Lord to embolden you. This is

not a time for meekness. It's a time for boldness, because in God's name you are commanding the light to act and commanding the angelic hosts to do battle for you. The light of God brings the power, strength, courage and boldness to deal with even the toughest of problems.

Building a Prayer Momentum

The angels need the momentum of our prayer energy to act on earth. Saying a fiat or decree many times over is not vain repetition. It's part of the science of using the spoken word in our devotions.

When you give a decree to Archangel Michael, you're filling your aura with his blue flame. That flame (its vibration and energy) embodies the qualities of faith, the will of God, protection and perfection. By giving the decree, you establish here below a magnet of the very qualities you desire Archangel Michael to bring to you. The greater your momentum of the blue flame, the greater your magnetization of that flame from the angelic hosts.

Repetition is the means whereby you build a momentum of light of a certain frequency for a particular purpose. And you can increase your momentum by praying daily and, if possible, at the same time each day.

When we call Archangel Michael into a situation—for instance, one that may involve thousands of people, such as drugs, terrorism, war or natural disasters—we may need to repeat the decree many times to build a sufficient momentum for the angels to act effectively.

> *A good prayer, though often used, is still fresh and fair in the ears and eyes of Heaven.*
>
> — THOMAS FULLER

The Powerful Prayers of a Shepherd

This is a story from a devoted student of the angels, a shepherd, who has a great momentum on decreeing.

One day while tending my flock up in the hills, I decided to give a mantra to the great Archangel Michael to protect the people of earth. I promised that I would do the decree many thousands of times, believing that the more I gave to him, the more he would help the people of earth.

While giving the decree, my physical body was surrounded by a large spinning sphere of blinding white light. Michael's presence was so ponderous that I could feel this archangel radiating tremendous power into the earth. At that point in time, I knew that he was pouring his power into the earth to benefit her people.

I completed my promise of decrees before the summer ended.

A Reservoir of Light

After giving decrees to Archangel Michael for some time, you may find that something in you changes, something locks in. You may feel a tangible flow of light through you. It may be like a whoosh of light and a sensation in your whole body. Your sense of struggle may lessen, and you may know that there is a clearing. And you may recognize that in that moment, your prayers, building a momentum of devotion, have opened the way for Archangel Michael to literally place his Presence over you.

This momentum, the accumulation of your devoted decrees, gives Archangel Michael and his legions the best opportunity to answer your calls for help when you need it. And it creates a reservoir of light sealed in your heart that you can draw upon in difficult situations.

 ## Fiats — Quick Calls for a Quick Response

Angels don't travel, not even by the speed of light. They materialize. They are. You say their name and they are present. If you want to call forth the presence and immediate help of Archangel Michael, give this fiat:

> Archangel Michael,
> Help me! Help me! Help me!

When everything seems to be going wrong, call to Archangel Michael's legions. Use the full power of your being to accept nothing less than victory every day of your life, and give this fiat:

Charge! Charge! Charge!
And let victory be proclaimed!

Multiplying the Power of the Angels

All heavenly beings have an Electronic Presence, which is their auric field and emanation. It is composed of forcefields of light that comprise the individual identity. That Presence can be duplicated without limit. So heavenly beings can appear to anyone upon earth or to a million people simultaneously.

Thus, you can greatly multiply the power of Archangel Michael and his legions. You can give decrees for every man, woman and child worldwide and see all of them being defended by this mighty archangel.

When you are invoking angelic protection, visualize all of heaven filled with legions of blue-flame angels. See the angels all around you and everyone you know.

When we give the decree "I AM Michael, Michael, Michael," Archangel Michael places his Electronic Presence over us. It's as though we are inside of him. If you are Archangel Michael where you stand, then nothing can get by you, because nothing can get by the power of Archangel Michael and his sword of blue flame.

I AM Michael, Michael, Michael!

I AM Michael, Michael, Michael!
I stand within his flame
I AM Michael, Michael, Michael!
By God's own I AM name
I AM Michael, Michael, Michael!
His faith ablazing here
I AM Michael, Michael, Michael!
His power and love so dear!

I AM Michael, Michael, Michael!
To light and love I bow
I AM Michael, Michael, Michael!
To defend the faith I vow
I AM Michael, Michael, Michael!
I enlist the light of men
I AM Michael, Michael, Michael!
America defend.

I AM Michael, Michael, Michael!
His shield of faith I wear
I AM Michael, Michael, Michael!
His circle and sword I bear
I AM Michael, Michael, Michael!
Enarmored by his love

I AM Michael, Michael, Michael!
Blue lightning from above!

I AM Michael, Michael, Michael!
Protected by his word
I AM Michael, Michael, Michael!
The Captain of the Lord
I AM Michael, Michael, Michael!
His legions now descend
I AM Michael, Michael, Michael!
Each child of the light defend!

 # Your Armour of Light

Giving the following decree, "Tube of Light," builds a powerful energy of protection around you. When you call forth your tube of light, see yourself sealed in an armour of light—a tube of fiery, opaque, white spiritual fire. See it descending from your I AM Presence and extending nine feet in diameter all around you and beneath your feet. See it blocking all negative energy directed at you. Then see the tube filled with violet flame, its spiritual energy liberating you from your burdens.

It's helpful to give this decree at the beginning of each prayer session to seal yourself in your own mighty tube of light protection.

To help your visualization, you can look at the Chart on page 62 while giving this decree.

Tube of Light

Beloved I AM Presence bright,
Round me seal your tube of light
From ascended master flame
Called forth now in God's own name.
Let it keep my temple free
From all discord sent to me.

I AM calling forth violet fire
To blaze and transmute all desire,
Keeping on in freedom's name
Till I AM one with the violet flame.

A Tangible Tube of Light

The tube of light can guard and seal us as we go about our daily lives. And it has provided great protection to people in the most dire situations. The following stories illustrate manifestations of the tube of light in both everyday and extraordinary circumstances.

One day I went shopping for some last-minute holiday food items. The parking lot was jammed and I was feeling overwhelmed. A friend had just taught me a short prayer and visualization for a protective tube of light. So after I parked, I sat in my car repeating the prayer till I could feel the light all around me.

Holding on to that feeling and image, I walked into the store. A three- or four-year-old boy was running straight toward me and the automatic sliding doors immediately behind me. While he ran, he was looking at the floor a few feet in front of him, unaware that he was about to crash into me.

Before I could step aside and before he saw me, he stopped short. Then, with an odd look on his face, he ran around me in a nearly perfect six-foot semicircle. I'm sure he either saw or felt my tube of light. Once he cleared

*it, he continued on his original course toward
the doors.*

———◆———

*T*his happened in Ghana during a time of
political unrest. Jacob, a member of the
government, was imprisoned along with
many others after the government fell. The
only thing he had with him in prison was a
leaflet of decrees that included the tube of
light. Hour by hour he gave the decrees
and visualized their action.

A time came when he and other inmates
were taken out before a firing squad. There
was a line of prisoners and a line of soldiers
with their guns. When the officer gave the
command to fire, all the prisoners fell dead
except Jacob. They reloaded and shot again,
and once more he was standing. And so they
tried a third time, and he still didn't fall.

Frightened, the authorities said to him,
"There must be something good about you,
so we're going to let you go." Eventually,
he became one of Ghana's ambassadors.

Jacob attributes his amazing survival to his tube of light.

 # Violet Flame of Joy and Forgiveness

One of the ways we can qualify light is with the violet flame—an extraordinary gift from God. In our physical world, violet light has the highest frequency in the visible spectrum. At spiritual levels, the high-frequency energy of the violet flame can consume debris within and between the atoms of our being. It has a transmutative effect—transmuting misqualifications of the light of God, transforming negative energy into positive energy. And it brings feelings of joy and freedom.

> *Forgiveness is the fragrance the violet sheds on the heel that has crushed it.*
>
> – MARK TWAIN

The color of the violet flame ranges from pale lilac to magenta to deep amethyst. You can imagine it working like a giant chalkboard eraser, wiping out feelings of pain, despair, suffering and limitation. See the violet flame passing through your heart to remove fear and doubt, hardness of heart, records of having withheld compassion to life. Sometimes you may also need to work on these things in psychological therapy. You can use the violet flame along with therapy to transmute the core and consequence of painful memories and experiences or anything else that you want to overcome.

You can invoke the violet flame by giving the following mantra. Try repeating it as you go about your day.

I AM a being of violet fire,
I AM the purity God desires.

See the violet flame transmuting all misuses of God's energy as you give the following decree.

I AM the Violet Flame

I AM the violet flame
In action in me now
I AM the violet flame
To light alone I bow

I AM the violet flame
In mighty cosmic power
I AM the light of God
Shining every hour
I AM the violet flame
Blazing like a sun
I AM God's sacred power
Freeing every one

The violet flame also carries the energy of mercy and forgiveness. The first step on the path toward God is to forgive ourselves and everyone else—all whom we have ever wronged and all who have ever wronged us.

If we really want to love, we must learn how to forgive.

– MOTHER TERESA

As you say the "Forgiveness" mantra, visualize spheres of violet flame going forth from your heart. See these spheres going to everyone you know, especially those with whom you have had discord and strife. Visualize the violet flame going to that person to bless him or her. Release all sense of injury and wrong into this flame. The violet flame can consume the cause, effect, record and memory of the wrong, reestablishing our hearts in the oneness of love. Repeat this mantra often and see how your life will change.

Forgiveness

I AM forgiveness acting here,
Casting out all doubt and fear,
Setting men forever free
With wings of cosmic victory.

I AM calling in full power
For forgiveness every hour;
To all life in every place
I flood forth forgiving grace.

As you qualify the light of God with the violet flame, you can send out millions of violet-flame spheres for the transmutation of the whole earth. This is the power of God in you. You can do something to change the world!

When Decrees
Won't Work

Decrees will not work for you if you have negative energy that you want to keep, because the angels don't interfere with your free will. So if you're determined that you're going to be angry at someone and you're going to hold on to anger, no angel will take it from you.

Maybe it's not overt anger you feel. Maybe it's just a slight sense of injustice that someone wronged you sometime, somewhere. Maybe it's irritation or mild dislike. Whatever it is, the angel who comes to help you with unresolved feelings can only take what you are willing to surrender into the mighty, flaming Presence of God.

You can pray to God and the angels for help in letting go of negative feelings. You can pray for the resolution of discord, misunderstandings and problems. Ask for guidance, ask for the help you need. And pray for oneness with the heart of God and the angels.

You can form your own prayer of the heart, and follow it with the forgiveness decree and other decrees to the violet flame. You may wish to say a simple prayer like this:

"Beloved angels, please help me to surrender this anger. Please send into my heart the flame of mercy and forgiveness, the violet transmuting flame. Let it consume all hardness of heart and nonforgiveness. And replace it with God's love and compassion. In the name I AM THAT I AM, I accept it done this hour in full power. Amen."

 # Everything You Do Can Be Sacred

Your life is sacred. Everything you do can be sacred. You can do decrees upon rising. When you step into the shower, you can give the tube of light decree and visualize the light pouring over you as the water comes down. This is spiritual ablution.

As you are dressing, you can give a mantra to the violet flame and see the blazing violet fire purifying your body, mind and soul.

On a small table in your bedroom, you can place a picture of the I AM Presence and a simple little cup symbolizing the chalice of your being. Then you can go there anytime to invoke the light.

You can call to Archangel Michael for protection for yourself and your loved ones as you prepare to leave your home, as you travel or go about your day, or as you retire at night. You can do this daily and build a momentum in your chakras and in your body temple of Archangel Michael's blue flame and all the attributes of that flame. And you can also do this with the violet flame or any of the other divine flames of God.

Then if a friend calls or comes to you and they are in need, you have a momentum of the attributes of that flame to transfer to them as well as words of comfort. It eases the burden, it transmutes the event, and it enables you to uphold them as they begin to put on the light and become more of their Higher Self, as you are also doing.

There is power in your voice—the power to create. By using your gift of speech, you can create positive changes in your life and in the world.

Reflections

1. What might you do to bring more sacredness into your daily life?

PART 7

True Stories of Michael's Intercession

The Littlest Ones Protected

The Miracle of the Canopy

Once you start praying and decreeing to Archangel Michael, you get a momentum on it. Through my prayers and decrees, I've established a heart contact with Archangel Michael. It's automatic for me to call to him. I rely on his protection and I feel his presence.

When this incident happened, I was living in a four-story brownstone in midtown Manhattan. One day I left my apartment and was walking down the avenue when an inner voice prompted me, "Go back to your apartment right now!"

I knew I hadn't forgotten anything, but I thought, "Okay, I gotta go back to my apartment."

Walking back, I saw my building in the distance. The nanny of the child downstairs was on the landing. She had the baby carriage, but she wasn't holding on to it. She had her back to it and she was trying to unlock the door. She didn't see the carriage start to roll towards the stairs—a very steep, 45-degree-angle stairway. It was almost like it was happening in slow motion.

When I saw the carriage rolling, I shouted, "Archangel Michael, help that little kid! Archangel Michael, help that child!"

The carriage hit the stairs and went boom! boom! boom! all the way down. When it hit the bottom stair, it flew forward and flipped. What happened seemed to be in defiance of the laws of physics. The canopy, which had been positioned at the back end of the carriage, flew forward faster than the carriage did. And the canopy caught the child as the baby carriage flipped over!

People ran up expecting, horror of horrors, to find the child badly injured. But when we lifted up the canopy, the child was just fine. There were rocks on the ground where the child's head would have hit had it not been caught by this canopy. I had just

witnessed a miracle. The child was fine.
It was an amazing thing to see!

I wouldn't get in a car or start the day
without calling to Archangel Michael for pro-
tection. Archangel Michael historically made
a vow to intercede and to protect us. Why
wouldn't I take advantage of that?

Over the Juniper Tree

Our *kitchen window has a direct view of*
our backyard where there is a good-sized
juniper tree. When my son was about two
years old, I usually gave prayers to Archangel
Michael before our day began.

One morning after I had given my
prayers, he was sitting in his high chair in the
kitchen facing toward the window. As I gave
him his breakfast, he looked out the window
and announced, somewhat matter-of-factly,
"There's Archangel Michael."

I looked out the window and saw only the
juniper tree. So I asked, "Where is he, honey?"

"He's over the tree," he said. And he kept
on eating.

All I could do was visualize in my heart and mind's eye the incredible presence of an archangel in my backyard, having answered my daily prayers, so very near and dear that a little boy could see him and calmly accept the reality of his appearance.

The Angel in a Suit

When I was young, I injured my leg very badly. I had three surgeries and had to wear a brace on my leg. My mother had three other children to also care for, so at times a Red Cross driver would take me to my appointments for physical therapy.

This one day the Red Cross driver had to make a stop at somebody's home. She parked on a hill—a great, long hill that ended in a very busy road. I sat in the car while she went into the person's house.

While she was gone, the car started to roll backwards down the hill. It picked up speed and I knew I was going to end up on that busy road. I knew I was in trouble, *and I was scared!*

Then the next thing I knew, a man opened the car door, got in and stopped the car. He was impeccably dressed in a light-colored suit and a tie and a white shirt. He looked tall and slim. He said to me, "There you are. You'll be all right now."

Then he left. That was it. He just sort of went. There was no man there before; and when he left, I really couldn't see where he went. He just left.

When the driver came out, her car was halfway down the road. I could tell that she was frightened. She looked at me like I had done something wrong, and she asked, "Did you touch anything in the car?"

I said, "No, I didn't. The car started to roll. I didn't know what to do. And then a man came and got in the car and stopped it."

I never thought anything of it until I was an adult. As a child, you expect some-body to rescue you, so that's what happened. As a child, you wouldn't look at the details.

We had picked up some speed and somehow this man got in the car very easily. He just opened the door and got in and pulled the emergency brake. But now I definitely think it was Archangel Michael or my guardian angel.

Archangel Michael around Town

Muggers Flee in Fear

*A*fter a late evening out in an unfamiliar part of the city, I ended up walking in a not-so-great area near the downtown. A gang of maybe eight young guys came out of nowhere and jumped me.

One guy punched me in the face really hard, splitting my lip and knocking me to the ground. Another was trying to find my wallet, and a third guy was kicking me in and about the head.

These guys were violent, full of rage. I thought I'd be left for dead. I felt, frankly, *that nothing would stop them from anything.*

I began calling to Archangel Michael loudly, "Archangel Michael, help me, help me! Archangel Michael, help me!

One of the guys said, "We don't give a bleep about your Archangel Michael."

Again I called out, "Archangel Michael, help me!"

I remember, just then, looking at one guy's face and seeing fear. Then, almost in unison, they all just fled. They ran!

There was no reason for them to feel I was a threat to them. I was on the ground. They had me where they wanted me. There was no reason for them to flee. They didn't get what they wanted, obviously—they didn't get my wallet.

When I got medical treatment and talked to the police officers, they almost couldn't believe a gang just ran away like that. I had to get stitches in my lip, but it healed pretty well. Other than that, I was okay.

I believe there was spiritual intercession, because there was no reason for those guys to have fled. It was fantastic!

Miraculous Survival from Bullet Wounds

When she was sixteen, Lucy had a premonition that she would die a violent death at age thirty. The feeling didn't go away with adolescence. At twenty-five, she began asking God to keep her from the death she felt was fated.

In the meantime, she had become a Montreal police officer. Although violence against police officers is rarer in Canada than in America, Lucy felt that she was in danger and asked God to lead her to prayers for protection. She had heard that Archangel Michael was the patron of police officers, so she was looking for prayers to him.

She was thirty when she first learned about decrees and prayers to Archangel Michael as well as the fiat "Archangel Michael, help me! help me! help me!" She quickly memorized the decrees and began giving them on her way to and from work and during breaks. "I was almost in constant communion with the angels," she recalls.

On May 22, 1993, Lucy gave two hours
of decrees to Archangel Michael before going
to work at 8 p.m. That night, she and her
partner were searching for an assault suspect.
They pulled up to someone and asked him
if he had seen anything. The man leveled a
9 mm pistol at them and demanded their
weapons. When they hesitated, he shot them
both—Lucy in the head, face and leg and her
partner in the head.

Lucy opened her door and fell out, trying
to take cover under the car. "Lord Michael!
help me! help me! help me!" she called
aloud. Her call frightened the gunman, who
ran away, thinking she was radioing for help.
This gave her the time to actually get to the
radio. (The gunman was later caught and
convicted.)

Although Lucy had been seriously
wounded, the bullets miraculously missed her
spinal cord and major blood vessels. She "was
probably within millimeters of having something tragic happen," said her surgeon.

Lucy attributes the near misses as well as

her swift recovery to Archangel Michael. She never went into shock. And she was walking around two days after the shooting. Ten days after that, she left the hospital. Although her hearing was impaired and some of her facial muscles were paralyzed, today she can hear, in the low normal range. The doctors originally told her that she would never again hear out of her right ear. Lucy calls her recovery "awesome!"

Why didn't Archangel Michael keep her from being shot in the first place? Lucy believes that her karma prevented him from stopping the bullets. But she also thinks that her prayers enabled Michael to redirect the bullets so that she was not killed. Although at one time her karma may have destined her to die at age thirty, her determination to live and her choice to pray changed her "fate."

"My karma didn't allow the bullets to be stopped, but what Archangel Michael did was just as good. He saved my life!" she said. "God doesn't always answer our prayers the way we expect him to."

Right in Their Cap

I live in Manhattan and I meet a lot of
cops. I tell them, "Look, you've really got to
pray to Archangel Michael before you start
your job each day. Call for protection for
the whole day. Ask him to intercede, come
what may."

Some officers say, "I know. Archangel
Michael is the patron saint of police officers.
I've got a picture of him in my cap."

A lot of officers keep photos of their family in their cap, and then there's maybe a little
card of Archangel Michael—right in their cap.

The Angel Shows Himself
in Pillars of Blue Light

I learned at a seminar that angels and
archangels do not come uninvited. One
thing that was said freed me forever from
orthodox religions' do's and don'ts: "You
don't have to believe what I am telling you.
You can make the call and prove the

law in your own life."

When I was walking home that night at about 1 a.m., I remembered that the outside light to the basement apartment where I lived was burned out. I had had a fear of darkness before, which I felt again that night. So I remembered to call to Archangel Michael to place his presence around me, to clear me from all fear, and to show himself to me.

When I arrived home, my outside light was on, but it was not an ordinary light. It was so bright I could hardly look at it. I don't remember installing a 1500-watt bulb outside!

I left that light on and went to bed. As I was trying to sleep, pillars of blue light kept appearing beside my bed. I remembered that I had called to Archangel Michael to show himself, but I was not expecting a light show!

Then I called to Archangel Michael to take me to his retreat at Banff, Canada, while I slept. That night I had a very peaceful sleep and woke up full of vitality.

Saved in the Stone Cellar

My mother had passed away in North
Carolina and I was about to leave on a flight
to attend her funeral. The morning that I was
scheduled to take the flight, I woke up with a
dream that showed me a dark rectangular
hole in the ground near my childhood home,
where my mother had lived. The warning in
the dream was quite clear that I was not to
fall into this hole. I interpreted it as my
mother's grave.

I had a timely errand to run before the
flight, and I thought, "I can do my Archangel
Michael prayers on the plane." However,
something inside of me said, "Do them now!"
So I offered my calls to beloved Archangel
Michael before leaving my home. Then
I hurried to do my errand.

I arrived at the building, quickly opened
a door and stepped into what I thought was a
dark hallway. It wasn't a hallway. It was the
entrance to a cellar. I fell headfirst down a

flight of stairs that led into a stone-lined
cellar and banged my head hard against the
stone wall.

The first thing I remember after that was
someone saying to me, "Can you move your
fingers?" I assured them that I could. They
helped me up and suggested I get medical
attention, so I did. And I thought, "Oh, they
think something might be wrong with me."

The nurses and doctor at the health center
were discreet. They asked, "Does anything
hurt? Can you see all right?" And they
asked if I had a bump on my head.

And I thought, "You know, I'm fine."
And then I began to realize that it was a
very serious accident that had happened,
a very serious fall.

I am profoundly grateful to Archangel
Michael, who saved me when I fell into the
dark rectangular space I had been warned
about but had not understood. I feel certain
that Archangel Michael has rescued me
more times than I know. And you can be
sure that I pray to Archangel Michael very,
very frequently.

Tragedy and Mishaps Averted

Archangel Michael Stands in the Way of Danger

I was driving on the freeway and a car was passing me. As it was moving in front of me, I could tell that it was going to hit the front of my car. I shouted, "Archangel Michael, help me!"

Instantly, I saw Archangel Michael appear between my car and the other car. He was huge. There he was, right there. There was no impact, no accident. Archangel Michael stood between the other car and mine to keep me safe.

Plummeting Car Reversed

It was early one winter afternoon in 1994 when I was driving with my wife and daughters to take the older one to the airport. There was snow on the road from the previous day, but the wind had blown most of it off the highway so that there were extensive areas of exposed pavement. The air was cold and I was not sure whether or not there might be some "black ice."

As we traveled on the straight stretch of highway past the canyon, I decided to test the brakes a little to see if there was any tendency to skid. The car immediately went into a slide, turned completely around in a circle and headed down the sloping embankment. In panic I shouted, "Archangel Michael!"

Immediately the car turned and went up the embankment and back onto the highway. I breathed a sigh of relief, grateful for his quick intercession. My wife exclaimed, "Good for you!" (for making the call).

I realized that this was a miracle that all of us had witnessed. How wonderful it is to have the intercession of the angels when it is most needed!

Saved within Seconds from a Collision

*L*ast January, I phoned my husband at work
to let him know I would be driving to a
nearby town to drop off my computer and
pick up a magazine rack. As always, I decreed
to Archangel Michael for protection on the
road. The eight-mile drive revealed slippery
patches on the interstate, not a hazard under
normal conditions.

When I got there, I loaded up the heavy
wooden rack in the back of our sedan, along
with a tire iron and other tools. Returning on
the interstate, I kept up with the 70 mph
traffic.

Suddenly a car appeared to my right,
forcing itself into mine. There was no time to
speed up or slow down, so I swerved sharply
to the left to avoid the collision. My car fish-
tailed perilously for a few seconds and then
instantly regained complete control. Cars
around me had braked and I could feel the
fear of the drivers.

As I drove home, I knew I had missed a fatal collision by seconds. Moreover, the heavy objects in the back of the car had plummeted sideways, but they hadn't hit the back of my head.

Once safely in our driveway, I phoned my husband to let him know what had happened. He told me that from the moment I had told him I was driving to town, he felt a strong prompting to decree to Archangel Michael for my protection. He said the pressure from the archangel was so strong, he had no choice but to decree. My husband had not stopped until I phoned him back. We both knew that the archangel had interceded to save my life that day.

Trapped under a Huge Truck— and Saved!

One day, Kelly and her friends Wayne, Russell and Heather piled into Wayne's compact sedan to go to a church picnic. The four teenagers had been decreeing to the angels for only a few weeks. They gave

Archangel Michael's "Traveling Protection" before heading off.

Just after they exited the highway and were on an overpass, a fully loaded 18-wheeler ran a red light, and then it plowed directly into their car. The huge truck dragged the car under its wheels for about 500 feet before stopping.

Kelly was in the backseat on the passenger's side—the side where the truck impacted. She was pinned in the crushed metal from the bottom of her feet to the middle of her chest. One wheel of the stalled truck was directly above her body and she couldn't breathe.

"Do your calls!" yelled Heather, who was also in the backseat. Kelly couldn't speak, but she made a silent prayer to Archangel Michael.

Strange as it sounds, Kelly swears that the truck instantly lifted a few inches, and this gave her time to twist the upper part of her body free. Then the weight of the truck descended again. "All of a sudden, I could breathe," said Kelly. Her first words aloud were, "Thank you, Archangel Michael!"

During the nearly two hours it took to get her out of the wreckage, Kelly said she remained "perfectly calm," comforted by the presence of Michael and his angels.

After three surgeries, Kelly still has some hip problems, but she says it's "nothing you couldn't live with." Wayne was uninjured, while Russell received a blow to his head and Heather a broken arm. Kelly says that she knows for sure that Archangel Michael saved them all from lasting injury or even death.

Michael Appears: A Radiant Youthful Warrior

It happened in the wee hours after a busy day at a conference I was attending. That night I had a vivid and terrifying nightmare. I was forcibly locked up in a deep cave with demons all around tormenting and torturing me. I could see my body sleeping on the other side of a wall of prison bars. I was crying out and pleading to my body to wake up, but to

*no avail. Finally, in desperation, I called to
Archangel Michael.*

*Instantly I was back in my body and
wide-awake. Sitting up in my bed, the fear
began to subside as I glanced around at famil-
iar surroundings. My roommate was still
sound asleep, but around his bed and mine
a blur of blue angels was rapidly pursuing a
shadowy mass. It soon left through the open
window and disappeared from sight, followed
closely by the angelic pursuers. This entire
process, probably taking no more than several
seconds, left me somewhat stunned.*

*Redirecting my gaze to the foot of my bed,
I then saw Archangel Michael standing there,
his golden hair wafting in solar breezes that
seemed to come from another dimension.
Holding his sword before him, he filled the
entire space from floor to ceiling. He had
the angular youthful face of a warrior and
large heavenly wings, and he was clothed in
brilliant golden armour—all radiating and
interpenetrated with a transparent, vibrant
cobalt blue.*

Within moments, my emotional state had

*progressed from terror, to relief, to surprise
and now to reverent awe at this magnificent
and privileged experience. I let my soul drink
deeply of the angelic vision as my eyes spoke
gratitude to his.*

*If a man's eyes are windows to his soul,
perhaps an archangel's eyes are portals to
the entire cosmos—past, present and future.
Every moment of man's strife and victory
seemed recorded in his ageless, radiant
visage. In his gaze, I felt comfort, peace and
transcendent love. No harm could ever come
to me with Michael as my guardian.*

*I did not see him leave. I know he never
will. I have only to close my eyes to see his
face and feel his power and love about me.
For this, no words can ever express my
gratitude.*

PART 8

Bringing Michael into Your Life

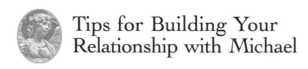# Tips for Building Your Relationship with Michael

1. Commune daily with Archangel Michael.

Take some time each day in prayer to speak from your heart. Share your hopes and concerns with this great archangel. And ask for help and guidance. Then listen quietly and be attentive to any direction you might receive.

2. Give assignments to Michael and his legions.

As you become aware of timely issues, perhaps while reading about them or watching the news, give decrees and quick fiats. Send Archangel Michael and his angels into these situations to bring about the best solution.

3. Be specific in your prayers and visualizations.

When you give the angels assignments, be as specific as possible, giving exact names. Visualize the blue lightning of Archangel Michael surrounding and penetrating the people, problems or situations you are praying for.

4. Daily use the spoken word, especially decrees, to anchor the light.

You can anchor the light of higher octaves through your daily prayers and decrees. Use your voice and the power of God's name to call for the light and to bring it into the earth through angelic intercession.

5. Amplify your prayer power.

Ask for your prayers and decrees to be multiplied and maximized for everyone on earth.

Repeat your decrees to build a momentum and reservoir of light that you can draw upon instantaneously when it is needed.

6. Have an image of Archangel Michael in your home and in your car.

As you look at his image in a picture or a statue, you can meditate on Archangel Michael and visualize him engaged in spiritual work. The physical image also anchors the light of Archangel Michael's presence.

7. **Do your part to keep yourself and your family safe.**

Take practical and commonsense steps for the safety and security of yourself and your family. Lock your house and car, keep your eye on your children. Get the professional help you need to deal with your physical health, psychology, legalities and other problematical situations. Archangel Michael can do more to protect you when you do your part in the physical plane.

8. **Obey the laws of God and man.**

Archangel Michael is the defender of the law. He is able to bring you his great protection when you observe the laws of God and man.

9. **Visit Archangel Michael's retreat.**

Before you go to sleep at night, call to Archangel Michael and his angels to escort your soul to his retreat while you sleep. Keep a notebook and pen by your bed, and write down any insights you notice when you wake up. (See page 26 for more about Archangel Michael's retreat.)

10. Tell others about Archangel Michael.

When you meet people who seem as though they could use some assistance from the angels, tell them about Archangel Michael. You might also want to give them a picture of him. Then they can have an image for their calls and as a reminder of the presence of this mighty archangel.

 # Be a Friend to Archangel Michael

As I was meditating upon Archangel Michael and contemplating with great joy the wonder of his presence, I realized that so many people pray to Michael because of what he will do for them, and of course this is lawful. But I thought, our dear Archangel Michael must need a friend, someone who will love him just because he is Archangel Michael and not only because of the favors he grants.

And so, I got caught up in the bliss of thinking how the offering that I might place before him would be the gift of friendship, of loving him for the great sacrifice that he originally made to be able to stand for you and for me.

I hope you will think about that when you are in the fast pace of life and have to quickly give your calls to Archangel Michael. Send him a real love message from your heart, a great sphere of light that asks for nothing except to simply pay tribute and to say, "Archangel Michael, I am your friend on earth. What can I do for you?"

My prayer for each and every one of you is that you will become the friend of Archangel Michael, and when you have need of a friend, he will be there for you.

ADDITIONAL RESOURCES

CDS AND IMAGES

**Devotions, Decrees and Spirited Songs
to Archangel Michael**
   by Elizabeth Clare Prophet
   1 CD with booklet introductory pace #D93090

Save the World with Violet Flame #1
   by Saint Germain
   2 CDs introductory pace #D88019

Archangel Michael (stained-glass portrait, see cover)
   wallet-size card, full color #3581

Chart of Your Divine Self
   2⅛" x 3⅝", full color #1060

BOOKS

How to Work with Angels
   by Elizabeth Clare Prophet
   Pocket guide 118 pages #4445

Violet Flame to Heal Body, Mind and Soul
   by Elizabeth Clare Prophet
   Pocket guide 100 pages #4424

To place an order or request a free catalog, please contact:
Summit University Press, 63 Summit Way,
Gardiner, MT 59030-9314 USA
1-800-245-5445 or 406-848-9500
www.SummitUniversityPress.com

SUMMIT UNIVERSITY PRESS®

POCKET GUIDES TO
PRACTICAL SPIRITUALITY SERIES

Elizabeth Clare Prophet, world-renowned author, lecturer and teacher, has pioneered techniques in practical spirituality, including the creative power of sound for personal growth and world transformation. Among her best-selling titles are *Fallen Angels and the Origins of Evil, Saint Germain On Alchemy, How to Work with Angels* and *Violet Flame to Heal Body, Mind and Soul*. A wide selection of her titles has been translated into 31 languages and they are sold online and in fine bookstores worldwide.